Employee Motivation

90 Minute Guides

Michelle N. Halsey

Silver City Publications & Training, L.L.C.
P.O. Box 1914
Nampa, ID 83653
https://www.silvercitypublications.com/shop/

ISBN-10: 1-64004-020-X
ISBN-13: 978-1-64004-020-5

Contents

Chapter 1 – Employee Motivation

Employee Motivation is becoming ever more important in the workplace as time goes on, and everyone agrees that a motivated workforce is far more likely to be a successful workforce. The happier and more professional an employee is, the better the results they will deliver for you. Of course, every employer wants to make sure that they have a workforce who will do their best, but this does not simply mean making the job easy for their employees. In fact, part of the problem of motivation is that where the job is too easy, employees become complacent.

There is therefore a challenge for all employers and management in delivering the right balance between a confident, motivated workforce and a workforce which is driven to attain goals. It can be described as a mix between the pleasure of a comfortable working environment and the fear of failure, although in honesty it is more complicated than that equation suggests. Regardless of how it is characterized, it is important to get the right balance in order to ensure that you have a motivated workforce. This manual is designed to show participants the way to get the best out of a confident, motivated set of employees, and to show them how to motivate that group.

By the end of this chapter, you will:

- Defining motivation, an employer's role in it and how the employee can play a part

- Identifying the importance of Employee Motivation

- Identifying methods of Employee Motivation

- Describing the theories which pertain to Employee Motivation – with particular reference to psychology

- Identifying personality types and how they fit into a plan for Employee Motivation.

- Setting clear and defined goals.

- Identifying specific issues in the field, and addressing these issues and how to maintain this going forward.

A Psychological Approach

The importance of psychology in achieving and maintaining Employee Motivation is essential. A message can be repeated over and over to a group of employees but unless they believe it and believe in it, the words are empty. The following are some of the key psychological theories which aid employers in their end goal of producing a motivated workforce.

Herzberg's Theory of Motivation

Herzberg's theory is that Employee Motivation is affected both by the employee's level of satisfaction and dissatisfaction and that, importantly, these two elements are independent of one another. That is to say that although an employee can be satisfied by the elements of their job which are intrinsic to the job itself, such as achievement and recognition, while at the same time being dissatisfied by the elements which are secondary factors of the work – pay and benefits, job security and relationships with co-workers.

This was described by Herzberg as the Motivation-Hygiene Theory. Elements which are done because they are essential to the job were considered the "motivation" part of the theory. They were done because they *had* to be done; therefore the worker was "motivated" to carry them out. Carrying these tasks out was considered to be the motivation of the employee, because they were required or compelled to do them. Having work to do demand that the worker rise to – and meet – a challenge, their motivation was set in stone.

The "hygiene" element, rather than a reference to personal hygiene and cleanliness as one might assume, was actually a reference to the upkeep of personal determination. They were things that needed to be constantly maintained because they were not intrinsic to the job. Herzberg's assertion was that the opposite of satisfaction was not Dissatisfaction, but rather an absence of satisfaction. Similarly, the opposite of dissatisfaction was an absence of dissatisfaction rather than simply satisfaction. In terms of motivating employees, it is important to encourage satisfaction on the one hand, and avoid dissatisfaction on the other.

Maslow's Hierarchy of Needs

Abraham Maslow's pyramid detailing the hierarchy of human needs is actually a more general listing of things on which every human should be able to rely on, but is applicable to the issue of Employee Motivation. In any job, from the most basic to the most specialized, the employee should be able to rely on their employer and their co-workers to uphold their access to the most basic needs – those which are essential and without which a human's health will suffer. The absence of access to these needs is the basis for everything else. As we go up the pyramid the needs become less essential but arguably more decisive.

A sense of security and of belonging is also important to any employee. Knowing that one's physical safety is ensured allows a person to do their job without fear. Security is not merely a physical concept; it also refers to the security of a person's job and the conditions that allow them to do that job. Giving a person tasks to do is an essential part of motivation, but providing them the environment in which to carry out those tasks is no less important for motivation. Allowing a level of interaction and encouraging a team ethic will further a person's intent to do their job and do it well.

In the upper two echelons of the pyramid, the needs are now more refined and specific. It is possible to do a job without self-esteem, but it is undesirable. Encouragement and positive feedback are important factors in ensuring that an employee does their job to the best of their ability. Without these factors, the likely outcome is a drop in performance and a reluctance to carry out further tasks completely and reliably. Self-actualization needs such as creativity and spontaneity allow the mind to work to its optimum level, and actively motivate the employee. These theories fit in somewhat with Herzberg's – that there are certain things which must be guaranteed as an absolute base, and then others which guarantee the effort of an effective employee through their desire to be part of something good.

The Two Models and Motivation

Abraham Maslow's theory on the hierarchy of human needs was an influence on Frederick Herzberg's later theory regarding the factors which motivate workers. While Maslow considered the needs of a person to all be on the one hierarchical list, Herzberg felt that there were two very separate elements of the plan. To look at Maslow's list, one would feel that as the requirements as set out in the pyramid were met, the level of satisfaction would rise while, at the same pace, the dissatisfaction would drop. It was Herzberg's contention that this is not the case. Herzberg felt that satisfaction and dissatisfaction were actually wholly separate and that both needed to be attended to.

Herzberg and Maslow created two separate theories, and while much of what is set out in the hierarchy of needs is backed up by the theories in the "two factor" theory, it is expanded upon and honed. While to look at Maslow's model one would feel that as long as certain needs were met, satisfaction would rise and dissatisfaction fall in equal measure, Herzberg holds that one could have a high level of satisfaction from carrying out their tasks in an efficient manner and meeting their targets, yet if they were constantly worried that they could lose their job for reasons separate to performance, they would not be as motivated as they could be.

There is, however, something to be said of Maslow's hierarchy, in that the pyramid as he set it out could be split into sections. In this case, the top sections (and particularly the peak) would correspond somewhat to Herzberg's "motivation" factors and the lower sections to his "hygiene factors. Herzberg's theory is not a contradiction of Maslow's, but at the same time is not a direct application of it. There are certainly differences between the two. They both have their part to play in employee motivation, however, and they have a lot more in common than to separate them.

Chapter 2 – Object-Oriented Theory

Motivation is not all about philosophical needs, of course. A lot of people work better when they have the concrete facts in front of them – something to work towards, something to avoid. Different things motivate different people, and in any given team or workforce there will be a mix of these people. As Herzberg's Theory suggests, what will motivate each individual will be a mix of satisfaction and non-dissatisfaction. This is similar to the old theory of the "carrot and whip" – based on the hypothesis of riding a horse and using the carrot to encourage it to speed up, and the whip to prevent it from slowing down too much. Then there is also the idea of the plant – seeing a worker as a "plant" who, given the right mix of the already-discussed factors, will flower beautifully. The carrot, the whip, and the plant are united into the heading of "Object-Oriented Theory".

The Carrot

The "carrot" as a theory takes its lead from horse-riding and dates back to the middle of the 20th century. The idea is that a cart driver would tie a carrot to a long stick and dangle it in front of the horse or donkey which was pulling his cart. As the donkey moved forward towards the carrot, he would pull the cart and driver forward, ensuring that the carrot always remained beyond his reach until such time as the driver slowed down and stopped, at which point – should he so desire – the driver could give the carrot to the horse as a reward for doing what it has been encouraged to do.

For the employer, this can perhaps be read in a number of ways. Looking at how the "carrot" theory works, it is quite easy to assume that the "carrots" offered to employees should be continually moved beyond their reach, and this assumes that the employee is as stubborn and witless as a donkey. This would be a rash assumption to make, and continually moving the point of reward away from the employee could be seen as a disincentive. Not delivering on a promise is always likely to annoy workers rather than stiffen their resolve to meet the new goals.

It could, however, also be argued that the carrot on the stick is something which should not just hang there within easy reach. The employee will need to keep testing themselves, but as long as they meet their challenges they will be rewarded at the end of their efforts.

In the theory detailed in the first paragraph, there is a defined end point. The important element of the theory is that if someone has the promise of a reward at the end of their work, they are likely to keep striving for it. If that reward is continually denied them even at the end of their work, however, do not be surprised if it ceases to work.

The Whip

In different cultures it is known by different names, but the second part of the "Carrot" theory is the Whip. There is a long history of terms and sayings attached to the idea of having an element of threat involved in motivating a group of employees, or anyone for that matter. "Spare the rod and spoil the child", for example, is an old proverb meaning that if you never punish someone for transgressing, they will come to believe that they can transgress as and when they wish. In the old "Carrot" theory, the way it works is that if the employee tired of chasing after a carrot that never seems to get any closer, simply slows down, a quick smack with the whip will make it speed up again.

The theory of motivation by threat of punishment is one which needs to be handled very carefully indeed. Not only is it absolutely illegal in many places to physically discipline workers, but other forms of threat can have a detrimental effect on the workforce. An employer, team leader, or manager with a reputation for flying off the handle when things are not to their satisfaction may get results from some people, but this method can lead to a culture of fear within a company or department, and stifle performance in order to simply get the work done.

It is left up to the person providing the motivation to decide to what extent and in what way they will use the "whip". There can be initiatives which combine the carrot and the whip – for example, in a one-off situation over the course of a day or so, the person or people who have performed worst in the team can be required to buy coffees or any other small reward for those who have performed best. A "forfeit" system can also be applied, but it is dangerous to apply anything too humiliating in this situation. The limits of the system need to be clearly defined. If it is something so meaningless that it won't be taken seriously, the whip ceases to be a motivation. If it is too stringent it becomes the whole focus and can infringe upon performance.

The Plant

An element of objected-oriented motivation which, is essentially separate from the above, but not incompatible with them, is known as "Plant" theory. Take as your example a simple house plant. In order to ensure that a plant flourishes it is important to give it the best combination possible of different nourishing elements. Most plants will require sunlight, warmth, water, and food in order to grow in the way you would wish. By the same token, employees will be motivated by a combination of factors.

The average employee will require motivation in many of the forms discussed by Maslow and Herzberg, and because humans are not all the same it will be a matter of judgment to ensure that each employee gets the right amount of each factor. This can be something as simple as getting the balance of "carrot and whip" motivation right. It is important, in many managers' eyes, to get the balance right between the arm around the shoulders and the boot up the backside. Making an employee feel valued and supported without letting them become coddled is important, as is ensuring that they know they have to perform without making them feel like they have a gun against their head.

Taking three of Herzberg's essential elements of motivation as an example, some employees work best with the prospect of challenge in their work, while some will work better with the goal of recognition. Others, equally, will want simply to get through as much work as they can while doing the work to a high level of quality. It is important to take into account the differing "buttons" that need to be pressed in each staff member to ensure that they do their job as well as possible. It is many people's view that the team which will work best is the one that has a combination of people who work well under different motivations. This way, tasks within the team can be assigned in a balanced way and ensure the best performance from every individual, and consequently the best performance from the team. The "Plant" theory, as applied here, is about knowing which plant requires which type of nourishment in which measure. By getting the balance right you can ensure the best "greenhouse" arrangement.

Chapter 3 – Using Reinforcement Theory

The concept of reinforcement theory is an old idea, which has been used in many different settings for many different purposes. If you have a pet dog, the chances are that you have used reinforcement theory in training it to behave the right way – a treat for sitting, rolling over and walking when you ask it to, and a punishment for climbing on the furniture or going to the toilet in the house. It is not, however, limited to dogs, although the way it is applied changes depending on whom the theory is being practiced on. For humans, something as crude as a piece of candy to reward a good deed will not be as effective, but the concept of rewarding good practice and punishing bad holds firm. Reinforcement theory has been established as successful and coherent, and it is a valid method of ensuring the best performance.

A History of Reinforcement Theory

We are all conditioned to act in certain ways based on certain stimuli. This is something that is visible in most things we do. From something as simple as waking up and getting out of bed when an alarm goes, to calling the fire department if we see a fire, our responses to certain situations are more or less instinctive , as we are not automatons, we do have some leeway in exactly how we respond. The knowledge of how we respond to stimuli was articulated in 1911 by E.L. Thorndike in what he called the "Law of Effect". Essentially, this lays down that in a situation where normal results can be expected, a response to stimuli which is followed by something good will become more "right" in our minds, while a response followed by something "bad" will become more "wrong".

To take this theory and apply it practically, as children we are still learning and our parents will usually use positive and negative reinforcement to apply lessons. Practically, if we eat up all our vegetable when we may not necessarily want to, we will be given a pudding after dinner. If we push our sister over, we may be sent to our room or to sit in the corner and think about what we have done. These reinforcement steps may be applied as often as possible until we always eat our vegetable and refrain from pushing our sisters over.

Behavioral conditioning is a subject which some consider controversial and even cruel, but there is a strong body of opinion which suggests that it is absolutely necessary. B.F. Skinner responded to arguments that human drives needed to be respected by saying that people learn behaviors based on what resulted from them. If somebody is of a mind to transgress because they enjoy transgression, but find that the result of their conduct is reduced freedom, they will become less likely to transgress so often. The thought of transgressing can become painful when associated with the idea of what will result. This theory is known as "behaviorism".

Behavior Modification in Four Steps

Once we have accepted that there is a truth to the theory of reinforcement, it is important to look at how the theory can be applied in terms of ensuring the desired behavior. The message of reinforcement theory is that it is possible for you to modify behavior in yourself or in others by associating undesirable behaviors with undesirable outcomes. In order to be fully "scientific" and guarantee the desired results from a program of behavior modification, it is worth following a strict pattern and recording the results faithfully. By referring to the results it is possible to see what patterns of modification work best. The following is a trusted four-step pattern for behavior modification:

1. Define the behavior to be modified.

2. Record the rate at which that behavior takes place.

3. Change the consequences which result from that behavior.

4. If this does not succeed in preventing the behavior, change the consequences to a greater or lesser extent.

By working through this model as often as is necessary it is possible to change the behavior of an individual from being detrimental to being positive in most cases. The form that this pattern might take practically in a workplace is as follows. *Person A has a tendency to leave their work station and go and speak to their friend, Person B. Person A is perfectly capable of delivering good work when they keep their mind on it. The distraction is infringing on Person B's work, too, and they do not have the willpower to refrain from chatting with Person A. In order to ensure that both people's work is as good as it can be it is necessary to stop Person A from behaving in this way.* Thus we have defined the behavior to be modified.

It is then necessary to see how often this happens. If it happens three times a day outside of scheduled breaks, and goes on for ten minutes at a time, then half an hour is lost to this behavior in a given day. If it is allowed to continue, this can build into hours lost in a given week – in fact, in a five day week, five "person hours" are lost to this behavior – half an hour each day for Person A and half an hour for Person B. As yet, nothing is being done. There are numerous things that could be tried here. Simply telling them to return to their workstation is one. If this works in reducing the amount of time lost, then a positive result has been achieved.

However, this may mean that Person A simply changes tack and goes to chat with their friend when you are not in the vicinity. Most offices now, however, have software which records the amount of time an employee stays away from their work station. By checking the time lost in a given day, and tallying the times that Person A and B were both inactive, it is possible to record how much time is lost when you are away from your desk. This can then be addressed in a number of ways. One way may be to stagger the lunch breaks of the members of the team, ensuring that Persons A and B cannot take lunch together as they would prefer. By checking how this affects the conduct of Person A you can see if this is working. As time goes on you can apply a number of different methods and settle on the one that works best.

Appropriate Uses in the Workplace

As things stand, it is really up to the employer, line manager or other supervisor to decide how to apply reinforcement and behavior modification in the workplace. The above example is one case where it can be helpful, but behavior modification is not limited to cases of deliberate transgression (although if the transgression is deliberate it will be more likely to build a clear, causal link in the mind of the individual). Behavior modification can also be used to aid a situation where an employee is working less effectively than they might for reasons other than rule-breaking. People have different ways of going about their jobs, but if one or more employees have a technique that is hindering their results, then behavior modification can form part of their coaching.

Reinforcement theory can also play a part in rewarding employees. If the members of a team have risen above and beyond what is expected of them, it is usually within the capability of a company to deliver some form of reward such as a team lunch. The knowledge that they can have a leisurely two-hour lunch break on the company if they consistently hit targets and exceed expectations is something that will remain in the minds of employees. They will be encouraged to continue the good work by the knowledge that their ability to exceed expectations has been noted and rewarded, and may be rewarded again.

Chapter 4 – Using Expectancy Theory

While there are a number of theories which focus on needs as a driver of motivation, Victor Vroom's Theory of Expectancy rather thrives on the outcomes. To clarify, while Herzberg and Maslow make the case for motivation being something that is dependent on need, Vroom suggests that the best motivation is to concentrate on the result of work as being the ultimate goal. He splits the process down into three sections – effort (for which motivation is essential), performance, and outcome. The theory is that if the employee is sufficiently motivated to achieve the results, their performance will be better as a result, and the outcome will to some extent take care of itself as a result of improved performance – which will itself be a result of greater effort.

A History of Expectancy Theory

Victor Vroom is a much-respected professor and researcher in the business world, and works at the Yale Business School as well as serving as a consultant for some of the world's most successful companies. This elevated status is due in no small part to his expectancy theory of motivation, which addresses the reasons why people follow the path that they do within corporations. His proposition was that behavior results from choices made by the individual where the choice exists to do something else. The underlying truth in this theory is that people will do what works out best for them. The important element is the outcome.

Vroom worked on this theory with fellow business scientists Edward Lawler and Lyman Porter. The theory dates back to 1964 and is still widely used by professors. While the process is characterized as **Effort, Performance, Outcome**, and more specifically as **E>P** (increased effort leads to a greater performance) and **P>O** (increased performance brings a better outcome), he takes notice of the fact that greater effort will not happen all by itself. What makes a satisfactory outcome for one individual may not necessarily work for another.

Clearly the theory has convinced many, as Vroom has been much in demand since the theory was unveiled, and major companies such as American Express have taken great care to solicit his opinions. While the Expectancy Theory may seem simple and largely self-explanatory, Vroom does make specific reference to elements which can easily be ignored, and without which the theory would not work. It is therefore beneficial to take not only the three factors above, but Vroom's three "Variables".

Understanding the Three Factors

The core variables in the theory of expectancy are Valence, Expectancy, and Instrumentality. The meaning that these variables have is as follows:

Valence – the importance that is placed by the individual upon the expected outcome. If the outcome for a project's successful completion is that the individual will be rewarded with more important projects when they would actually rather be rewarded with time off, they will place less value on the outcome, and their motivation to perform well will suffer, leading to reduced effort. Ensuring that the valence of a task is at a suitable level is a significant motivation

Expectancy – the belief that increased effort will lead to increased performance. Expressed in more simple terms, this means that if you put in more effort, the results will be better. This obviously depends to some extent on having the resources, the skills, and the support to get the job done. While effort is undoubtedly important it is not quite accurate to say that more effort will always mean better results. More effort on its own may well simply be wasted effort, if the person doing the work is using the wrong tools, is the wrong person or is working with people who have limited interest in reaching the same outcome.

Instrumentality – this is the belief that if an individual performs up to a certain level, they will be rewarded with an outcome that will be beneficial to them. It is one thing to tell an individual that, should they meet their performance targets, they will be rewarded with a beneficial outcome, and another to convince them of that. The important factors in Instrumentality are:

• an understanding that performance equals outcome (so the reward depends upon the satisfactory performance)

• a sense of trust that the people who promise the reward will deliver

- trust in the capacity of the people judging the performance and the outcome

Therefore, the Theory will only work in practice if the individual recognizes that they need to perform, and trusts the people in control to judge their performance and deliver what is promised.

Using the Three Factors to Motivate in the Workplace

The three factors of the theory of expectation as set out above all have their part to play in the workplace. Along with what has been learned from Herzberg and Maslow's theories, we can take their insistence on the needs of an employee and put them in a goal-oriented context by applying Vroom's theories.

Firstly there is the issue of valence. Does the motivation exist to complete a task well if the outcome is uninspiring? Surely not, therefore to ensure the maximum motivation, it is ideal to offer something which will be coveted. This is perhaps the most important level of the E>P>O equation. The effort will rise to meet the outcome. How this is used in the workplace will depend on what the company can deliver.

Then there is the issue of expectancy. Effort will only lead to performance where the conditions exist to make it so. In the simplest terms, you might be able to deliver a fine reward to someone who can build a kennel for your dog. But if you only hand them two planks of wood and a broken screwdriver, you may as well offer them a trip around the world for all the good it will do. You cannot expect someone to meet their goals if you do not present conditions which make this possible. All the effort in the world will not make it happen.

Finally there is the issue of instrumentality. This is important in workplaces where big rewards have been offered before, and in those where it is done for the first time. There is little point in a small-income business to offer a sports car as an incentive for better performance, as there is little likelihood of them delivering it. Equally there is limited reason to offer a chocolate bar as the reward for a project which will make a company a million dollars, as it just seems like a slap in the face. Equally, if rewards have been offered before and the task completed only for the company to express their regrets and fail to pay out the reward, the chance that people will trust enough to put the effort in again is greatly reduced.

Chapter 5 – Personality's Role in Motivation

In any organization, there needs to be a mix of personality types. The importance of personality types is decried by some as a kind of fad science, but it is difficult to run an office or any other workplace when everyone has the same "soft skills". The reason for this is perhaps best explained by the old saying "too many cooks spoil the broth". Where everyone has the same personality type and a problem arises, there is likely to be conflict as everyone tries to take the same role in solving it. The different personality types are not explicitly defined, and therefore there is no hard-and-fast list, but there is a set of soft skills which all workplaces require, and these are best met by different types of people.

Identifying Your Personality Type

You probably have an idea of your own personality type. A personality type is defined by the aspects of your character that emerge when around others or when doing important work. These character aspects are, as often as not, described as "soft skills". You may have been described as "maternal", "skeptical", "humorous", or any number of other things. These are issues which do not relate directly to your work but can aid or restrict your ability to do it, and can aid or restrict others. It is considered beneficial to have as many different types of personality in a workplace as possible.

There are countless tests that can be done to detect a personality type, and many different ways the results can be expressed, but there are certain things which hold true in all personality tests. Perhaps the best way in the workplace to detect a personality type is to judge your reaction to a problem which affects a whole team, or a group within it. Are you immediately looking for a way of overcoming the problem? Are you instinctively worried by what happens, and do you look to other people to help out? Do you comfort people who are stressed out by the problem? Or do you perhaps sit on the fringes, making comments and playing for laughs? Strange as it may sound, all of these elements are worthwhile in a team. The person who immediately looks for the solution is a "problem solver"; the second type is a "consensus seeker". The third is considered a "nurturer" while the last listed is a "humorist". All of these are classic personality types.

Equally, all of these people, and others, play a major part in making up a workplace.

- Without the problem solvers, an organization would be in trouble if things deviated from the plan as laid out.

- Without consensus seekers, it would be easy for a problem solver to become too autonomous, solving the problem to their satisfaction without being particularly concerned for how others felt about the solution.

- Without the nurturers, people would feel that a problem could too easily become a crisis.

- Without the humorists a bad situation would depress everyone.

Reason and etiquette dictate how much we allow our personality to take control of us, but most people will avoid becoming too "cliché" in how they behave. What is your personality type?

Identifying Others' Personality Type

Most people know, or have an idea of, what personality type they conform to most. When meeting new people – and the workplace is one arena where this happens perhaps more than any other – it can be difficult to get a handle on what other people's personality types are. The only way to really get a firm sight of what kind of personality you are dealing with is to speak to people and to monitor how they conduct themselves. One way of doing the latter is to hold "ice-breaking" or "getting to know you" games and sessions. By playing certain games and by monitoring people, you can find out a lot about what kind of person they are.

There are countless games designed to find out about people, one of which is the "stranded on a desert island" game. This basically takes the shape of a hypothetical shipwreck where the team is stranded on a desert island after their ship has run aground. There is a list of things which have been left on the ship, and limited time before the tide comes in and takes it away, so you have to prioritize what you will rescue, from the small, seemingly insignificant things to the larger items which may seem to have more practical use. Different people will wish to rescue different things, and will make their reasoning known. This game is beneficial because not only does it show what people's priorities are, it will also show a lot about their personality when you step "outside the game".

There will initially be a team of people sat there with lists which differ hugely. The whole team will, though, need to decide what they as a team rescue from the ship. In doing this, team members will make their points and some ground will be given on some items. From this you will be able to work out who is a dominant character, who is pragmatic, who is light-hearted, and so on. Some people will concede points quickly whereas others will try to make their point – whether they do so in a bullish way, a more structured way or however else. You will also find that in many situations two or more people will vie for the "Alpha" role, while others will value their less confrontational part. From games such as this you can learn a lot about someone else's personality type.

Motivators by Personality Type

The different personality types have different ways of motivating the people around them as well as themselves. Someone who emerges as a conciliatory person is likely to motivate others by speaking to them one-on-one and allowing them to see where they excel as well as where they can improve. Being able to put bad news in a good way, as well as being able to share good news discreetly in a way, can be very valuable.

Other people, who may have a more dominant personality, will have a different way of motivating positively or negatively. They will generally tend to prefer delivering criticism one-on-one, as doing it in the open will de-motivate others, but good news will be delivered loudly and shared throughout the team, as a way of spreading the joy and motivating other people to try to achieve the same, and gain the same kind of acclaim.

Depending on someone's personality type, they will have vastly different ways in which they can contribute to the team's motivation. Indeed, it is becoming common practice in many workplaces to have what are known as "champions" to take control of certain aspects of the team. This empowers people in non-management roles to play a significant part without pressuring them with the responsibility of the concrete performance of the team. By assigning people the correct champion's role, you can enable them to get the best out of themselves and others, and not let a talent go to waste.

Chapter 6 – Setting Goals

It is universally accepted that a business will get nowhere without having targets and ambitions to which to aspire. There is a phrase often used which describes people as "goal-oriented". The meaning of this phrase is that the individual seeks to achieve goals and defines their success by the reaching of these goals. If they fail to meet it, they consider that they have failed overall, no matter the quality of the work they have done to get there, or any obstacles overcome. Though this seems a little negative given the numerous ways in which a person can fail to reach their goals, it does not mean that having goals and aiming for them is not a valuable way to work.

Goals and Motivation

Anyone in a job will have some targets to meet with regard to their performance. The extent to which they achieve that, the number of times they do so, and the quality which they apply is all considered worthwhile material for target setting and attainment. Some companies set business-wide goals, while others set individual goals for each of their employees. Whatever the case, these goals are used in a number of ways, and are considered an important part of every job.

One way in which goals feed motivation is the obvious one of performance-related pay. While just about every job will come with a basic salary, the importance of ensuring that work is done to a satisfactory standard means that bonuses and top-up payments are paid out for achieving and surpassing goals. This feeds into people's need to be financially rewarded for doing a satisfactory job, one of the major motivations for working. If you feel that you are undervalued in your job, one complaint you may have is that it does not pay well enough. Therefore it is important for your employer to motivate you by paying you well enough, and for you to ensure you are well paid by meeting goals.

Another way in which goals aid the motivation of employees is that they introduce an element of competition. In most offices these days you will see a "results" board which carries the names of team members and their performance in set categories. Depending on how seriously you take competition, you may feel that being top of the list is the important thing – or that being ahead of a specific individual is more important. Regardless, no one wants to be last, and the public displaying of goals can make sure that people do their level best to perform – after all, as Herzberg contends, recognition is a major element of motivation.

Setting SMART Goal

It is one thing to set goals, and another to set meaningful goals. Anyone can set themselves an easily achievable goal, and meet it without really trying. This is not beneficial for motivation; by the same token it is non-beneficial to set goals for someone else that they simply cannot attain. The result of doing this is that they will fail to meet these goals and be discouraged. Rather than striving to meet them next time, they are as likely to exhaust themselves through futile effort or to let their frustration overcome them and fall ever shorter. It is important, to set intuitive goals which, though achievable, are not in any way guaranteed. This increases the challenge while keeping the real possibility of success.

Managers are now using an acronym to sum up the criteria that goals need to meet in order to be worthwhile, and calling them SMART goals. The acronym has various meanings, but for the most part the elements fall into the following categories:

Specific: Goals need to be definite and defined. They need to be on a level where only people who are prepared to work hard will achieve them.

Measurable: Goals need to be something which can be assessed and plotted against previous months and fellow staff members. They need to be worthwhile, and to constitute something that people will be proud to achieve

Achievable: There is no point in setting goals arbitrarily and unilaterally. Setting goals which a member of staff cannot achieve is counter-productive, and may have the opposite result from that intended

Realistic: As mentioned before, there is no point setting goals that cannot be achieved or which are too easy to achieve. They should not be set in regard to a minor element of the job, and achieving them should have tangible benefits.

Timed: Setting a goal of selling 100 units is relatively meaningless unless you specify a time period. Also, during the time period it should be possible to check in and see if the candidate is set to meet their goals or miss them.

Evaluating and Adapting

Based on what we have seen above, the importance of goals is not only in setting them in the first place, but in learning from the experience of achieving or missing them. Sometimes what looks like a realistic goal can be difficult or impossible to reach in the current situation and either the goals need to be re-set or the employee needs to be retrained or coached. Sometimes the goals will be achieved easily and ahead of schedule with a minimum of effort, in which case they may well need to be revised upwards or the employee's methods scrutinized. What is certain is that realistic and accurate goals can be used to evaluate an employee's performance and to see where changes can be made.

Based on an employee just narrowly missing their goals a few months in a row, it may be possible to find out one factor which is holding them back and preventing them from achieving what they are capable of. It may also be that they are hitting all but one of their targets, but just failing on the final one. In these cases, a target or goal can be used as a way of motivating the employee. If they can just hit that last target, then they will be rewarded. There are ways that they can improve their performance on that front, so they know what they need to do in order to hit it. This can be a very useful tool in ensuring that people take their training to heart and are motivated to apply it.

What can be said for certain is that misapplied targets and goals can have a detrimental effect on employee motivation from either side. Too easy and the employee becomes complacent, too hard and they become frustrated. This is why it is necessary to set SMART goals for an employee, and to fine-tune them if they cease to be SMART.

Chapter 7 – A Personal Toolbox

Motivating yourself and others is something that takes no small amount of effort and can sometimes seem like a fruitless endeavor, as motivation initiatives do not always take hold immediately (or at all, in some cases). It is also worth mentioning that, although there are many resources on the Internet for managers and team leaders seeking to motivate their employees, not all of these will work in a specific situation. It is well worth reading the best books and the best sites in order to promote ideas, but the best motivational strategy will always take some account of the exact situation where it is used, so it is worth honing yours somewhat.

Building Your Own Motivational Plan

A dedicated and specific motivational plan pertaining to the circumstances in which you are trying to motivate workers is a smart move. There are countless motivational plans and structures already in existence, but one of the reasons that these motivational plans have been successful is that they were designed for specific situations. Therefore, they may not work as well in your situation. They will most likely be beneficial, unquestionably, but they could be more so if you tailor the plan to your specific needs.

A good motivational plan will take account of a number of things: the identities and personality types of the people to be motivated; the time available to implement the plan; and the resources available to push the plan forward. Recognition of the parameters within which you must work is important. Few motivational plans are "one size fits all" in nature – and the ones which are will be of limited success because, they have to be less specific than they should be. A plan can be as intricate or as simple as you want to make it, but remember that the time you invest in it will be repaid by the results you get from using it.

This does not mean that you need to start from scratch and construct your own motivational plan from the ground up. There are some templates you can use, and a number of example plans on the Internet which can be taken as a guide from which to build. In these cases, it is important to look at the elements which are transferable and those which are not. The ones which are not should then be replaced by elements which are relevant to the situation in which you wish to implement a motivational program.

Encouraging Growth and Development

Development is something that is demanded by just about every section of our society today, and the workplace is absolutely no different in this respect. An employee who is new in the workplace will not offer the same skills and understanding as someone who has been there for five years, but will certainly bring some of their own qualities including a fresher outlook. The employee will change with time, and this is to be encouraged. It is also to be encouraged that they have some input while they are new. The benefits of this are twofold. Firstly, the new member of staff is encouraged to feel part of the team, and an important part at that. Secondly, the business benefits from a fresher outlook on things.

In order to encourage a new member of staff to grow as part of the business, it is worth listening to them and finding out where they see themselves fitting in. This will help in encouraging their development as a member of staff and as a person, and it will not solely benefit them. The more integrated a team is, the more smoothly it will work. The better people work together the more motivated they will feel to continue. A lack of personal motivation for the job is one of the main reasons that people look to find work elsewhere, and a business is never helped by losing its more able members.

The importance of growth and development in a business does not lie solely with its newer members. The fact is that you can teach an old dog a new trick, and the processes of development need not have an absolute end. Some people are of the opinion that once you cease developing it is time to give up. There is some truth behind this assertion, as development is a necessary by-product of challenge, and once a job has ceased to present challenges, it is difficult to retain your motivation.

Getting Others to See the Glass Half-Full

A major part of motivation in the workplace has to do with ensuring that people are not discouraged by situations which are anything other than favorable. The very definition of a challenge is that it is a situation which presents some risk of failure. For many people the fear of failure can be troubling. The challenge is in getting the fear of failure to represent as something different – the desire, the need for success. Fear of failure should not be a de-motivating factor. It would be surprising for most of us if we were not to some extent scared of failing – no one wants to fail, and this fear can provide the impetus for us to make sure we succeed.

More than anything, turning a bad or potentially bad situation into a good one relies on outlook. The way that this is normally verbalized is by asking whether you are a "glass half-full or a glass half empty" person. This is in some ways just a more simplified way of separating optimists from pessimists. Optimists look at a glass of water which contains exactly half its capacity and say that it is half-full, while pessimists look at it and say that it is half-empty. The more people you can get to maintain a "half-full" mindset, the better for staff motivation.

There are various ways to get people to see the glass half-full. Most common among these is in knowing the fact that challenges come with consequences and rewards. If you do not meet the challenge, you fear the consequences. If you do meet the challenge, you eagerly anticipate the rewards. The challenge is part of the job, so there is really no point in shrinking from it for fear of the consequences. Keeping the rewards in mind is a way of seeing the glass half-full, and makes it far more likely that you will live up to the challenge and have a chance to share in the rewards.

Chapter 8 – Motivation on the Job

The importance of motivation in any workplace is clear to see. Without motivated employees, any manager or team leader will find it a lot harder to get results out of their team. One can produce a fairly reasonable standard of work without having great motivation, but to exceed expectations and achieve great results it is essential to have superb motivation. Without something to concentrate on as the reward, the reason you do the job and the reason you *want to* do the job, it is difficult to produce quality results, because an absence of enthusiasm will always result in flaws.

The Key Factors

Over the course of this workshop we have looked at various factors in motivation, and philosophies of motivation as put forward by great minds of the business world. The key factors of motivation are diverse, and can come from anywhere. You may feel more motivated by the prospect of the punishment of failure than you do by the rewards of success. Even if you are motivated by the trappings of success, there are several different elements that can be covered by this – a higher salary, a promotion, the recognition of co-workers. Human motivation is something personal and cannot be second-guessed.

The inherent factors in motivational tools are that they fulfill a priority for the person concerned and that they can be relied on. If you want to provide motivation to a group of workers, it is essential that you allow for the fact that different workers will be motivated by different things. A company can spend as much money as it likes on tools for the job and on office facilities, but if the employees are not motivated on a personal level there is simply no point. Giving the employees reason to come in in the morning and do their job to the best of their ability is the only way you can guarantee the optimum level of performance.

Many of the factors that need to be considered with a view to motivating employees are those listed by Herzberg, Maslow, and Vroom. Employees need to feel secure first and foremost. They wish to feel secure in their job, and also in their personal life. If they are well enough remunerated they will be able to meet their rent or their mortgage payments. Employees also need to feel that they are valued and respected. But as well as how an employee feels, it is also important to consider what they covet. As often as not this will be a higher salary, better benefits, and the chance to take part in occasions which recognize brilliance.

Creating a Motivational Organization

An organization is only ever as strong as its employees, and a group of employees will only be as strong as its weakest members. In order to produce the best results over and over again there is nothing more important than ensuring that motivation is high throughout the organization. This means that a company needs to have a policy for motivation if it wants to have the best results. Good motivation from top to bottom is not something that can be achieved simply by flipping a switch, nor by decree from one boss. Good motivation is achieved by team members knowing that their work is appreciated and will be rewarded, and that they are valued within their organization.

Ensuring that this is the case entails a process of selecting the right people for the right jobs. Someone can be an excellent worker in terms of their knowledge of the procedures and tools required to perform operations, but if they are liable to have a corrosive effect on team morale then their position has to be considered. It is all well and good to be able to carry out your duties, but if when you are not carrying them out you insult team mates and create a hostile atmosphere then the overall effect will be negative for the company. To ensure a motivational organization it is essential to prioritize the appointment of staff that can work with others, provide encouragement or advice, and contribute to a positive working environment.

This is a question which comes down to balance. If you have an organization which has its fair share of problem solvers, consensus builders, nurturers, and humorists among others then you will have a far greater chance of creating the motivational environment that you are looking for. This is something that should be checked for at the recruitment stage. It is important to get people who can do the job, and it is also hugely important to get people with whom you and other people can work. A motivational organization is one in which the employees naturally complement one another as personalities and as workers.

Creating a Motivational Job

Ideally, any employee in a company will be able to reply to the question "Do you like your job?" with a "yes", a smile, and a list of reasons why. We have all heard, or read, or have been that person who is never done complaining about their job when not in the office, so it would appear that there is still some work to be done before we are all doing our perfect job. If perfect is not possible, then, we are looking for jobs which make us feel motivated, and as though we feel it is worth going to work tomorrow. Jobs like that do not grow on trees, but when you are a manager it is up to you to put the right job description together in order that potential employees feel that they want to do the job.

Everyone has their own perfect job. The idea of a perfect job is that it will be one that the employee will be happy to show up for, and which they would consider doing even if they weren't being paid. Although the simple truth is that most of us only countenance doing our job because we know that there is a pay check waiting at the end of it, it should be a target for everyone to have a job where they require little extra motivation beyond that which already exists – a target for employers and employees. If you have a happy workforce you are much more likely to have good work done.

So while people will generally find it very hard to ever get hold of their perfect job, having a good motivational job is something worth aiming for. The perfect motivational job is one which combines as many of the business philosophers' essential factors as possible. It will present challenges for the employee, but ones which are achievable for a diligent worker. Achieving these challenges will be met with financial and social reward and the confidence of maintaining a place in the business while also being recognized as a strong worker. In the best motivational jobs, an understanding will exist between the employer and the employee that each knows what the other is looking for, and can provide it.

Chapter 9 – Addressing Specific Morale Issues

Motivation in a job is linked intrinsically to morale. As interesting and challenging as work may be, if there is a problem with morale then it can very quickly run through the business and lead to underperformance. There are many reasons why morale may be low, and they range from the banal to the very serious. It is only by knowing the nature of the problem causing low morale that morale can be restored and the performance of the business resurrected to a high level. Low morale can affect an individual, or it may go wider than that. It can end up affecting an entire team, department, or company. Depending on what causes it each situation may require a different solution.

Dealing with Individual Morale Problems

Every employer has seen at least once in their time as the head of a team or company an employee who is suffering from low morale. Morale is the mental state of being confident in one's purpose, and is therefore most relevant in the workplace. Low morale is usually not difficult to identify, as it is usually visible in an individual's entire bearing, and then in their work performance. There are so many different factors which can affect morale that second-guessing the reasons why a particular staff member is unhappy can be very difficult. How you deal with the issue of an employee's low morale can easily govern how well they perform and how their morale goes from there.

On identifying an employee with low morale it can be a tricky situation to address. Everybody has their low days and these can happen for any reason, even for no reason. Sometimes people just "wake up on the wrong side of the bed". If you are concerned that it may be something more than that – if the colleague is showing signs of visible distress or appears not to be "switched on" for a prolonged period – then it is worth asking them how they are. This can be something as simple as stopping on your way past to ask "Are you OK?" in a relatively conversational tone. Generally people will not want to make a big deal of it, but it is important to ensure that they are looked after and aware that the help is there if they need it.

If the problem of low morale continues over time, it will clearly become detrimental to the employee and the employer. From a point of view of employee motivation as well as a sense of camaraderie, it is vital to ensure that every avenue is explored to ensure that the morale is lifted and the employee satisfied. It may be that they are concerned about their ability to do the job, and it may be something entirely unconnected to the job, but whatever the case it is essential that the employee should be able to see that there is available support there for them. If this support is not forthcoming, the morale problems can continue and spread. If it is, however, the team morale can be raised as a result.

Addressing Team Morale

Ask any sports coach, and they will tell you that a team assembled expensively from the finest players on the planet can be beaten by a team of scrappers from an amateur league if the professionals are short on team morale. Some of the most extravagantly gifted sides around rarely win anything because they fail to operate as a team. Meanwhile, sides who have players of limited ability can win trophies, as long as everybody works together and sacrifices their individual gratification for the collective good. In short, team spirit is vital to team performance. The way that people work together is governed by how they relate to one another.

In many workplaces, a team will be made up of ten or more people. This means that there are several different dynamics within the team, including those between each individual member, between groups and so forth. Having good team morale depends on ensuring that the separate team members are well-enough disposed towards one another to be able to work with them. If there is conflict within a team, it is certain to affect morale for some of those involved, and those who are on the outside watching it. For a team manager, the challenge is to ensure that this is avoided.

A manager can affect team morale being proactive or reactive, and can contribute to its building, or its destruction. It is essential in cases of team conflict to be even-handed and fair. Even if one does not feel this way they must be seen to be impartial. Favoritism must be avoided at all costs, and you need to be prepared to be unpopular in the short-term. It is much better to put your personal loyalties aside in order to ensure that individuals within the team are not alienated.

Petty conflicts can be over in days, but a reputation for bias sticks for good.

What to Do When the Whole Company is De-Motivated

A motivated workforce is absolutely essential to a successful company, and if there is an absence of motivation in just one part of the company it can affect results negatively. If that lack of morale spreads, or a lack of morale arises generally within the organization, then things will be much worse. The worst of all is when an entire company becomes de-motivated, and this can happen for a variety of reasons. The implications of this happening are that people will lose interest in their work, the company's results will drop, and people will begin to fear for their future employment.

An entire company can become de-motivated for a range of reasons. Perhaps the most obvious of these is that a company seems set to go bust, leading to mass unemployment of its members of staff. While in some cases this may galvanize the workforce to work harder in order to ensure the company's survival, market forces dictate that when a company is facing bankruptcy or liquidation it will be extremely difficult to turn things around without outside investment and a lot of luck. The mere prospect of unemployment can be enough to de-motivate the majority of a workforce. Other reasons why an entire workforce may become de-motivated include the loss of an important member of staff or an unpopular change in working practices.

When an entire company loses its motivation for any reason, this falls under the heading of "emergency" and action is required immediately to prevent it from becoming terminal. It falls upon the leaders of the company to sit down with the employees under their jurisdiction and speak seriously with them, offering complete honesty and answering all questions. Being realistic is absolutely essential in this respect. Just saying "there is no problem, everything is going to be OK" will convince no one. Admitting that there is something wrong and outlining how it will be overcome will encourage employees and even those who are initially unconvinced will have the chance to see how it will work. Nothing short of this kind of urgent action will prevent a workplace-wide loss of motivation from becoming terminal.

Chapter 10 – Keeping Yourself Motivated

Maintaining personal motivation is something essential as an important member of a company, particularly in the case where you are responsible for the motivation of others. As a team leader or manager you will be looked to for reassurance and guidance in a job, and if you give the impression that you are merely going through the motions, your lack of motivation can become contagious. Even if you are responsible solely for yourself, personal motivation remains vitally important. Motivation is what keeps us from giving up and refusing to get out of bed in the morning. Any way we can improve on our level of personal motivation is valuable.

Identifying Personal Motivators

What constitutes a motivation for one person may not be the same for others. Personal motivators are different between people, because the very definition of personal requires that you see things differently from the next person. The importance of identifying your own personal motivators is clear. Without a clear, identifiable set of personal motivating factors, it can be easy to fall into either an unmotivated condition or to rely on other people's motivations to keep you going forward. There are times when we cannot rely on other people to give us the motivation we feel we need, and when you are on your own you need to motivate yourself.

Identifying your own personal motivators is something that takes some self-knowledge and some thinking time. What is it that you want to take from your job? Are you happy to keep cashing the pay checks, or do you wish to advance further in the company? Why did you apply for the job in the first place – and are you close to satisfying that goal? Ask as many questions as you can ask yourself, and as many answers as you can give to those questions, the better your own personal motivation.

One motivation that works well for a number of people is surpassing themselves. Keeping a record of personal achievements attained while in your current job and attempting to do better every month is a challenge that is never completed. If this fails to motivate you, then look at other things which reward performance. Often, people are most motivated by the recognition of their achievements by others, and by setting an example to other members of staff. Whatever works for you is a valid means of self-motivation. Make sure that you have as many motivating factors as you can think of, because the more things you want to achieve, the more you will achieve.

Maximizing Your Motivators

As far as motivation in a job is concerned, it is a matter which requires regular evaluation and frequent updating. There are countless potential motivators for individuals, and as long as they work for you they are valid. What some people struggle with is ensuring that they continue to work. Particularly if you have been in the same job for a long time, it can be easy to lose the urgency and motivation that drove you to your best results when you started. Think of yourself ten years ago and the principles you held which you believed to be as solid as a rock. Do you still feel the same way now, or has life given you a different outlook?

Constantly giving some thought to what motivates you and why will enable you to get the best out of your motivators. When you started in the job, it may have been about the money, but maybe you have enough money now. In this case, it can help to think of something that you want to do which will require more money – taking a break to travel for a while, building a new house, or whatever suits your means. This is a way of maximizing an old motivator which may have ceased to be that effective. Maybe one of your motivations has been recognition. In this case, seeking to mentor a newer member of staff can be beneficial. While you may have achieved almost all there is to achieve in this job, someone else could maybe do with the benefit of your experience.

Taking the factors which have motivated you in the past and updating them for the future is one way to maximize your motivational factors. In addition, it helps to look at your home life as it relates to your work life. If there is something you really need or really want in your home life, and your job can help you achieve it, then this may be all the motivation you need. Pushing yourself to achieve as much as possible will eventually pay off, especially when other people have ceased to push you because they know how good you are

Evaluating and Adapting

We all have things which motivate us – when we are kids, when we are young adults and when we are mature adults – and all that changes is the nature of our motivations. Even once we have retired, we will often find that there are things that we need to do and need to achieve before we can truly rest. In fact, one thing that motivates a lot of people is the need to keep their minds active. Research has proven that people who remain active through their middle and early old age keep syndromes such as dementia at bay for longer than those who do not. This makes it all the more important to remain motivated.

It is sometimes too easy to just let things pass you by through complacency, especially when you have already achieved enough to make you more or less immune from being fired. While it may be nice to remain in a job even when on auto-pilot, there is no denying that it is disadvantageous for keeping the challenge in a job and for motivation. Should you want to make a move into another part of the company or another job, it is always useful to have a results sheet which shows continuing improvement and achievement. To this end it always helps to have a record of achievement and keep testing yourself against it

In the end, the person who can best judge how well you are doing is you. Any manager to whom you answer will probably have other people to manage as well, who may require more careful handling than you. The only way you can ensure you remain motivated is to motivate yourself – so if you find that your motivation is beginning to wane, look at other reasons to stay in the job and work harder. There are always reasons to push yourself, and it is a matter of finding the one which does it for you, no matter how often that changes.

Additional Titles

The 90 Minute Guide series of books covers a variety of general business skills and are intended to be completed in 90 minutes or less. It is an effective way for building your skill set and can be used to acquire professional development units needed by project managers and other industries to maintain their certification. For the availability of titles please see

https://www.silvercitypublications.com/shop/.

No. 1 - Appreciative Inquiry

No. 2 - Assertiveness and Self Control

No. 3 - Attention Management

No. 4 - Body Language Basics

No. 5 - Business Acumen

No. 6 - Business and Etiquette

No. 7 - Change Management

No. 8 - Coaching and Mentoring

No. 9 - Communications Strategies

No. 10 - Conflict Resolution

No. 11 - Creative Problem Solving

No. 12 - Delivering Constructive Criticism

No. 13 - Developing Creativity

No. 14 - Developing Emotional Intelligence

No. 15 - Developing Interpersonal Skills

No. 16 - Developing Social Intelligence

No. 17 - Employee Motivation

No. 18 - Facilitation Skills

No. 19 - Goal Setting and Getting Things Done

No. 20 - Knowledge Management Fundamentals

No. 21 - Leadership and Influence

No. 22 - Lean Process and Six Sigma Basics

No. 23 - Managing Anger

No. 24 - Meeting Management

No. 25 - Negotiation Skills

No. 26 - Networking Inside a Company

No. 27 - Networking Outside a Company

No. 28 - Office Politics for Managers

No. 29 - Organizational Skills

No. 30 - Performance Management

No. 31 - Presentation Skills

No. 32 - Public Speaking

No. 33 - Servant Leadership